RHYTHM SALES

Improving
Sales Performance and Wellbeing

PETER ANDERSON

DEDICATION

Lucia

CONTENTS

SALES ACKNOWLEDGMENTS

Rob Madge, Peter Marks, Crag Dunn, Samual Sims, Dave Smith, Nick Major, Kit Patel, Isabella Robins, Josh Harding

INTRODUCTION

To succeed in life, you need three things:
a wishbone, a backbone, and a funnybone.

Reba McEntire

I place my education boxes into the boot of my car. Taking a moment sitting behind the steering wheel, I reflect on the challenges I had to overcome with the young minds of the secondary school I had spent the day educating. I start the engine and see that my fuel gauge is almost empty, so head towards the nearest petrol station. My mind still planning my learning intervention for the next day, I top up the car with £10 worth of fuel knowing that my bank account is getting low. I engage in some greeting pleasantries as I walk towards the kiosk to pay for my petrol. I place my hand into my coat pocket, pull out my card and insert it into the card machine. I entered my pin. The sound of the card machine rattles as it produces my receipt. The man behind the counter respectfully shows me the receipt, which had the words, DECLINED in capital letters printed on the paper.

I panic. I don't have any other cards, and I have no money in my wallet. My heart rate accelerating, I search all my pockets. Negative self-talk starts to cloud my mind and the words "you useless shit" echo in my head. Desperately rummaging around in my inside pocket, my finger tips sense a paper-like object. Could it be? I pull it out from the inside of my jacket pocket and there staring up at me is a neatly folded £10 note. Relieved I pay for my fuel and as soon as possible, pull into a quiet side road. The tears roll down my cheeks.

I had reached my all time financial low. I couldn't afford my rent, I was unable to support my children, unable to treat my girlfriend and I spent endless days away from home working on a zero hour contract for education.

I was physically and emotionally crushed. Paralysed by my inability to make enough money. I felt I had so much to offer, but lacked an avenue to express my education and experience.

I had retired from a successful twenty-year career in the performing arts, re-educated myself with an MA in Leadership and Change and attempted to run my own business. I found out the hard way that being an artist and an educator are uniquely different skills from those needed to run a business.

In an act of desperation, I went looking for any stable job and walked up and down the High Street asking for any available vacancies. To my surprise, without any prior experience in retail, I was offered a job in sales with a furniture company.

Simultaneously, a local theatre offered me a job running the dance department. The dance position would have warmed my passion compared to furniture sales. But the dance wage was far lower than the furniture company's pay. For the first time in my life I surrendered to my need for money and took the job in sales. My heart broke. More tears, but this time while telling the theatre employer I would not be taking the job, which was slightly embarrassing. Now my negative voice is calling me "a loser and a wimp."

Starting my job, I was curious why, with no retail experience, I had been hired. The manager told me that the sales trainers could not teach people experience, but they can teach people to sell. I had plenty of life experience and my potential to be a great salesperson was waiting to be awoken.

For my artist soul, it was like a prison sentence. Doors slid open to the entrance of the store, allowing gusts of air to waft across our faces while we waited for the next punter to walk in with the need to buy. The door reveals a large car park full of vehicles taking people to the outside world, but I could not step out into that arena anymore. I had to watch my numbers. Numbers became my fixation in every moment of the day.

A colleague of mine asked what do you see when people walk through the door? I said, "people wanting to buy sofas." He said, "no you see money, and that money puts food on your table." Although I was unable to separate the person from the money, it was my first lesson that brought money into the equation. The airy artist and educator were about to be infiltrated by a drive and hunger for money unknown to my normal existence.

I had no particular yearning to sell, just a desperation to get out of my debt and hold a sense of self-dignity. And so the grafting and crafting began.

The pressure was on. I wasn't like the average sales person starting a new sales job. I had never even held a card machine, never talked to customers on the phone, I was 'formaphobic,' and the finance documents flooded me with stress, whilst the product knowledge seemed to be endless.

I received some clarity on why finances had crushed me before, when completing a sales qualification. I had to complete a BTEC in customer service in sales. It was an academic exercise which I had fun with while some other people in the store struggled. It turns out that I got the highest marks in the country for my writing. I find this paradox interesting because I can't get close to my colleagues on sales results, but I can write well about it.

There it was, the difference between understanding and experience. Experience is king/queen. I had more writing experience, so I excelled next to someone with less writing experience, although they were more skilled in sales.

I needed to get down on the floor and drown myself in experience so that the old me was no longer. Some of my colleagues had been selling since they left school and had crafted their style of selling. I observed how different personalities found various channels to get the deal done. Each sales artist had their way to success. I no longer saw it as a prison but now as a martial arts Dojo. A training arena to facilitate the birth of a new talent.

I had become a sponge asking for more knowledge, and the team was very supportive. I focused on observing the experts and role playing. I made many mistakes but kept getting up and moving forwards and slowly the perseverance paid off as products I could never sell before, became easy to sell and my sales figures rose. I am a bit of a research geek so I made notes as I went along. As I changed from not being able to sell to being able to, I recorded my progress. This recording meant I could look back at the change and understand the developments that had taken place.

When Complacency Sneaks in...

It was interesting to see how once I became confident with selling a product or service, complacency appeared and started to erode the excitement. And with this erosion, some of the magic slipped away. Somehow the words disappeared that used to swing the deal. I found myself lost to the reason why this had happened. Then the sales numbers started dropping. The mind began its desperate investigation to try to figure out what to do, what must I stop? What was it that was working, how could I bring back my mojo?

I have seen many a good sales person spiral into the abyss of helplessness. Being on commission-based pay means that one of the toughest challenges you face is when you don't make a single deal in a day. You may have been in the building for twelve hours and not a penny is in your pocket. As the mind becomes more wound up, the further away your possibilities of a deal become. There is a healthy relationship between your thought process and the sales you manage to close.

The ability to regulate your emotional state is one of the most important skills to master in sales. If you cannot leave a moneyless day at the front door, you'll end up taking your baggage with you into the next. And if you share a home with someone, this can cause difficulty in your relationship, which in turn leaves you deflated and trapped in a poor me mentality at the start of a new day. You have now created a vicious cycle. To get out of this cycle, you have to find a place to become centred, to remove the storm clouds from your mind. If you do not set your emotional state as a priority, your sales numbers can drop.

I have put together my experience from being in a place where I could not sell. Then I looked at how I began identifying and feeling the change in my mind as I started to see myself as a salesperson. This new identity as a salesperson did not need to be that person who forces products on others, but more of a advicer. The goal began to create mutual bonds that would leave others, as well as myself, feeling better for the human connection and I would be energised for the next sale. I thought I was forced to give up on the art world because of finances. As I advanced to the new chapter of my life, I found an artist living within the sales process. This realisation was the catalyst for my sales method. It gave structure and balance to the fundamental basis of selling and brought the necessary awareness of taking care of yourself. It was in the blending of my identity as a salesperson, educator and performer that the artistry of making money was realized.

The moment I realised I had found a method was when we were asked to sell a product that I didn't believe in, because it was over priced. It clashed with other products that served well enough in my mind. I had to take the emotion of it. People may want it, and I have to make sure I don't get in the way of the process. I evaluated what was working from the success of others and put my creative spin on the sales pitch. Although I thought the product was overpriced and not needed, within eight weeks, I was top of the store for selling this new product.

My training took over two years and helped me gain a sense of sales confidence. I took many knocks and bumps and struggled as I redesigned my neurology so that the artist and educator could also become the salesperson.

This book is for those people who have struggled to make money. They need to sell, but don't want to and need a reliable structure to act as a scaffolding within a sales environment. It is for those people who are not interested in the hard sell and are passionate about human relationships. This book is intended to help achieve the balance between driving for a deal, evolving as a sales artist and taking care of your ethics - all while making money.

I have built the structure of my method around the acronym RHYTHM. For me, this word is a dynamic blend of desire, creativity and self awareness. It is like keeping an eye on the scorecard, while empowering common good feelings. The RHYTHM Method allows us to dance within the complexity of sales, and fulfill our aspirations to achieve.

Mastering the mundane, repetitive activity of sales by integrating it as an art, can breath new life into the process. Crafting this skill encourages the sales person to re-adjust and motivate themselves to continually get better.

Learning never stops. When it does, the artist is gone, and a shell is left.

What I learned is that beyond sales techniques, of which there are many, there is also a necessity to be resilient, to be able to take care of yourself through the ups and downs of the emotional rollercoaster ride that are demanded of the body and the mind.

The RHYTHM Sales Method incorporates technique and self-care into the sales process.

1. How to create relationships with others and connect with them emotionally.

2. How to maintain a sense of self-care, most especially of your mental state.

The six stages allow these two complementary interactions to create results that generate more money and motivation into your life.

Below is a breakdown of the RHYTHM acronym.

The following six letters define each chapter of the book.

R. Relationship

People buy from people, and authentic relationships are one of the most powerful drivers in making money.

H. Highlight the Need

There are times when people are unaware of how a product or service can improve their lives. By investigating the underlying meaning of their words, you can offer products that can benefit them. This realisation can gave birth to a desire for the product.

Y. Yes and…

This creative exercise supports a positive mindset. It builds on the ideas that are being discussed and encourages an agile thought process while interacting with people.

T. Training

You need to understand your products and yourself. Your pitches need to be rehearsed to become second nature. Your product knowledge needs be mastered. And most critically, you will continually learn about your internal state and your external environment, in order to build the necessary emotional resilience for the rollercoaster of sales.

H. Humour

A sense of humour helps connect, makes the job more enjoyable and leaves a 'deal' with a feeling of saying goodbye to a new friend. This connection also helps further business deals in the future.

M. Mindset

Being mindful of how you interact with your client, as well as your psychological process, is essential for your overall well-being. In a culture that is drowning in work, it is important to see how we can stay mentally healthy during the challenges of making money.

It is my hope that my story will help others on the journey to improve their lives, and that they can integrate the RHYTHM Method into their work, but also their relationships and their play.

I am not the same person that I was before I dived into the world of sales. I resisted selling because I believed it involved deceiving and controlling others. But as I moved into it, I added a new skill to my toolbox, which will be with me forever. It is now a strength that helps build the life that I now believe I deserve. It is my hope that while you test elements of this method, you too will begin to feel your behaviour change, as you reframe old ways of thinking that might have limited your ability to make money.

If you are to embrace this new thought process, I hope that it will deliver the life that you deserve too.

Relationships

One of the most beautiful qualities of true
friendship is to understand and to be understood.

Lucius Annaeus Seneca

Whenever I have had a successful sales interaction, there has always been an underlying quality relationship. People buy from people they like. We are emotional beings, and this needs to be the platform for the sales interaction, rather than the objects of the trading process.

I have heard endless stories of people going to buy a product that they wanted. However, because of a bad experience they refused to purchase.

Although the sales person sees very little of the money, we subconsciously believe that we are doing business with that sales person. The rest of the company's branding and marketing disappear into the eyes and demeanor of the sales person.

The more we can relate, the stronger our bond becomes. We seem to have better experiences if we have shared stories, created meaning and laugh together throughout the transaction.

However, it has to be an authentic relationship; our senses are wired to recognise manipulation, which means honesty has immense power. This being understood, as the connection grows, the conversation still needs to be directed towards closing the deal.

In this section, I will delve deeper into the nuances of bonding with your client and the ideas to keep at the forefront of your mind.

Common Ground

I once met a senior man in the store, someone who everybody else seemed to be avoiding. He was 'offish' and showed no desire to connect emotionally with anyone else.

I enjoy these types of challenges and went and sat next to him. We started talking, and he had a thick London accent growling the little dialogue he was willing to share with me.

I asked him what part of London he was from? "South London," he replied. I decided to take a chance and made a joke. I informed him I could not serve him because I was from the north of London and it would be dishonourable to my tribe to cross the river and sell to him.

He cracked a smile, and we had a laugh about the two sides of London. We were now connected and entwined in conversation. Our chat led to building our relationship to a point where, when it came to his buying the product, he was open to suggestions that I happily gave to him.

It is important to take the time to find common ground before moving forward with the deal. Otherwise, you end up backpedaling to gain a sense of trust from your client or customer.

Shared Meaning

The smallest of offerings can bring a human connection closer, but establishing a deeper connection can be achieved through shared meaning.

I remember once I was selling for a charity and I met this young businessman. He was not willing to give a donation to our cause. It was a clear "No, thank you." But I took a moment. I told him that it was not a problem, but I shared with him why I found it so valuable. It was for a child's education company, and I shared with him that I was dyslexic. I struggled at school, but I was able to get through with guidance from dedicated teachers. This support, in turn, led me to develop my gifts. So when I sell for this charity, I believe that I am giving another person the opportunity to break through their struggle and the possibility of living their dreams.

To my surprise, he openly admitted that he was also dyslexic. He had had terrible trouble at school. When he left, he formed his own business and now earns more money than most of the people that bullied him for his 'stupidness.'

We had a silently "shared meaning" of our struggles and what it meant for other people that may also be struggling. In a sudden shift, he changed his mind and gave a donation.

If there is an authentic reason to sell something that is meaningful to you and you can communicate this with somebody, there is a higher chance that you will inspire that value in your product. This value increases the likelihood of the client investing.

A Foundation of Feathers

The power of small acknowledgments within relationships are built on a foundation of feathers. What I mean by this is that the little offerings that you give express kindness and softness. The attention to care creates a sense of safety for a stranger to communicate more openly with you. The continual attention to such subtleties can give way to a greater influence than one large gesture of goodwill.

I remember making somebody a coffee that seemed to be having difficulty walking and looked like her back was stiff. She was indecisive. I opened up many questions to help her narrow down her possibilities. The store was empty, so I took the time understanding the discomfort she was in while uncovering the product need and desires that she had not yet formulated. She went away, and there was no sale at that moment. Later that day she returned saying that she had been to all the surrounding stores and I was the first person she felt was not pushing a sale. I was the one she wanted to buy from, and she was ready to sign the contract. On reflection, I had not realised that during my authentic concern for her wellbeing I had created a real sense of trust. This confidence had helped her chose the company she wanted to give her time and money to.

Pear Shaped

Fondness can be of great benefit when circumstances outside your control do not go well. Taking the time to acknowledge and connect with your client may give you the necessary emotional deposit to bank for a rainy day.

I once had a client who had purchased a product thinking that it would fit into her home. However, something was overlooked that prevented the product from fitting into the house. This meant we were going to charge the client for a re-order due to a measuring error.

Her partner was military and was furious to return to this headache from a tour of duty. However, thanks to the emotional credit we had established through our relationship, we were able to overcome the blip.

In these moments of anger, it is so important to get inside the mind of the client and understand their frustration and pain. Communicating my understanding clearly and authentically, meant that the situation had a higher possibility of being diffused. When the raw emotion softened, we had a chance of looking at the facts of the situation and seeing what action we could take. This conflict ended in spoilings of sugary doughnuts and a thank you for the time and understanding given. In addition, they left with a promise to continue doing business with us.

Salespeople are in the business of selling emotions, so taking time for rapport and shared meaning creates the platform for your relationship. Creating this fondness makes the sales process more rewarding. And gives you the foundation to investigate the client's needs:

- People buy from people
- The more we can relate, the stronger our bond becomes
- Find common ground
- Uncover shared meaning

Highlight the Need

A shy gem is our vulnerable need. When it catches the sun, it sparkles giving birth to our desire.

Peter Anderson

In sales, it is essential to uncover the need of the person to whom you are selling and to highlight the level of desire sitting within it, as well as any potential obstacles to overcome.

Today many companies have to upsell their services which can leave specialists without sales training struggling with their sales pitch. Recently, I visited an optician to buy a new pair of glasses. The optician was trying to upsell me from a basic frame to a superior one. I could feel him stumbling with his language as he tried to improve the sale. He had not asked any questions around my desire to have new glasses.

I wanted something a bit fancy. Something special for when I give my workshops and I was willing to pay extra for that. The optician's sales-stumbling almost forced me to buy a cheaper pair of glasses. If you advise without painting a clear picture of the person's needs, you can instead create a feeling of being misunderstood. This jumbled information can have a client leaving unsatisfied which, in turn, can negatively affect the possibility of return business.

Questions

Questions, especially open questions, are valuable tools for investigation. There is an artistry to delivering questions. If your questions are listed routinely, they can become journalistic, without creating a conversation of equality. This invasive "prying" can be irritating to the listener, and close the relationship doors. By looking for the what, why, when, how and where, you can instead gently create an emotional picture from their personal information. If they can get to ask you a few questions, and you share some of your life with them, this can create an even deeper sense of reciprocity. However, while keeping a conversation open and exciting the focus must remain on navigating the subject, and the subject must be the journey towards the sales objective. Keep under the umbrella of relevance.

Your questions are forming a collage of meaning that can tell you the story of the person's needs. Later on in the sale, you can refer to this mental imagery to smoothly deliver solutions to the now highlighted needs.

Start the conversation with gentle questions that are about the environment or noticing something in the moment. This questioning is a mental warm-up before delving deeper into the pool of understanding. Just like when you go swimming in cold water, jumping in too quick often leads to a shock and coming out just as fast screaming. Be too invasive to a client, and they will be screaming in their head to get away from you as soon as possible.

Four areas of sales investigation can be:

1. The person's environment: i.e. what area they are from

2. Their relationships with people close to them

3. The passions that they are involved with in their life: e.g. dancing

4. What are their behaviours at the moment linked to the product. In other words why are they buying the product now? What problem does it solve?

Questions are a great way of diffusing assumptions. How many times do your tastes and experience get in the way of another person's wants and needs? I have sold many a painting which I perceived unworthy of the asking price. But by asking certain questions about their perceived meaning and the way the client lights up emotionally, tells me they are far more interested in the painting than I would every be. Seeing this shift of excitement in their body means I have to forget about my views, add more emotional kindle to their interest and blow enough energy into the fire to create a burning need for them to buy.

Opening Barriers

Objections can be barriers that are put in place because of a lack of information. There are times when an open question can create a realisation for someone. It's as if you open the door to a view that the customer never previously knew existed. In this instance, it may take time for the client to reflect on these new possibilities. It can help if you support this process that is taking them from the past thought to the new one.

This confusion happened with a client when I suggested some add-ons to their order. It was not something they had budgeted for, and the evidence I was using to support this did not show accurate understanding. Thinking they could be more of a visual person I pulled out a pen and begin to scribble down the idea in a visual drawing. This sketching led to the right understanding and I was able to proceed to closing the deal. Many of us are not audio learners so giving other opportunities to understand information can be very useful and help provide clarity for new suggestions.

Question Bank

It is ideal to start with a list of set-up questions. This list is like a question bank, designed to release the questions that lead to the product. These repeated questions become like your performance routine, one that always has the sale in mind. I normally have three questions that are designed to open up the pathways towards the sale. These can give me permission to look for the needs of the person.

It can feel robotic at times, almost as if you are blagging your way into the deal. However, if it is coming from the heart, it is far better to have rehearsed questions than having a blank stare on your face as you try desperately to find something to instigate a connection.

However there can be challenges to training this questioning behaviour, but making them a habit shows great results in sales outcomes.

Shut the F**k Up

As humans, we can get excited about talking about ourselves. If you are like most people, your own thoughts and experiences may be your favorite topic of conversation. According to Adrian F. Ward, people spend on average, 60 percent of conversations talking about themselves. Research shows the reason is because it feels good and can benefit personal growth, individual happiness, and social bonds. It is the job of the sales person to activate this feel good factor in the deal.

As the ancient proverb says: we have two ears and one mouth - do more listening and less talking.

When you have unraveled the need, give the customer time to make sense of their own information. They may need to ponder the idea of purchasing something they had not planned. I was once taught, I must "shut the f**k up," when a customer is contemplating a purchase. Although a crude teaching technique, it did imprint the need to create space. This space is a sensitive moment for the customer, and any pushing can repel the person away. It is important that the final decision is theirs, resulting from all the investigation and advice you have given.

Giving respect to customers creates reciprocity and your likeably factor rises. Not being liked reduces your sales potential.

I overheard a story about somebody who wanted to buy a car. They knew what car they wanted and decided to buy it from the local car dealers. After talking to the sales person who was very pushy and demanding they decided to walk away. He wanted the product, but he said, "there is no way I'm giving that w**** my money." This frustration is a reminder that people sometimes see the exchange of goods linked to the person selling, rather than the product itself.

Put the breaks on, slow down and get to know your customer.

Delicate Words

Questions can also spark emotions and so the ability to be a delicate wordsmith with a sensitive touch with language, can make a world of difference.

I like to go to cashiers to get my shopping done. I find the beeping metal boxes of the self-service machines very impersonal. The smiles and personal connection of social interaction feeds my day.

However, one day I bought a reduced microwave meal from the discounted section of a supermarket that was about to pass its sell by date. As I reached over to grab a bag, the cashier noticed what I had bought. "That's a cheap deal you got for your food," she mentions enthusiastically. The emphasis on 'cheap' made me feel that my food was off and that I was selling-out on my dietary needs. Deep down I was guilty I had microwave food. When I returned to the store, the slight negative discomfort I had experienced, steered me away from the humans. I veered towards the self-service, so I could be undisturbed in my little guilty bubble with my special food deals. Although this example is quite petty, it shows the amplification of our insecurities from the choice of somebody's words.

Feel the Love

We often think that decisions are based more on reason, but behind most rational thinking and walls of intellect, are emotions.

I have seen many customers struggle with the idea of practicality of one product versus the love of another. The love tends to be the emotional need showing itself. By emphasising their stronger emotions, people tend to feel more satisfied when purchasing a product bought from the heart. Customers tend to connect desire with the better quality product. It is by giving reassuring support for their love of the product that you can help direct the decision-making.

I had a customer who was allowing the behaviour of their pets to be the deal breaker of a product. By the way they held tension in their bodies, I could see physically that their decision was going against the desire of the better product. When I could delve deeper and understand their relationship to the passion of the product, it became apparent that some behaviour patterns were dictated by their pet and needed to change. They decided to create boundaries through basic dog training, and now these customers were able to treat themselves to a dream purchase, a purchase that they had wished for some time. So in this example, I had to bypass the practical need and delve into the emotional need for them to buy a product that they would be happy with for many years to come.

Validating people's decisions as they go along the sales process is helpful. Your attention can give people the feeling that their opinions are valid and worthwhile. Even if you do not agree with somebody and their choice and you would prefer to shout out "what are you doing?" it is important to remain objective. Recognising customers' feelings towards a product and highlighting those emotional states, helps compound their action toward the tipping point of the sale.

Social Benefit

Needs can have a wider spectrum than just the initial and personal emotional state of the purchase. If your company supports good causes, the client can be made more conscious of where they place their money in relation to a social benefit. A business that provides fair trade can influence based on compassion. What are the social consciousness needs of your buyer? Does your product tick your client's wish box for a cause that is important to them.

To know that at the end of a deal the profits of the company are not only in the shareholder's pockets, but also affecting a wider social community, can add real value. It is important to share all the positive repercussions that will come from the person purchasing your particular product or service.

Surfing the Tantrum

Emotions convene like the seasons shifting from one climate to the next at great speed. In a moment we can feel that we are in a sunny place. One trigger and we are in a thunderstorm. Just like the seasons, if we ride them out, the weather will change. Clients' emotions will lose their charge if you can help them name them. A neutralised space will come, but you may have to wait out the negativity first.

One of the ways to ride such a wave is to keep a detached awareness of the client's need. Being pulled into the client's negativity can be far more strenuous than sitting back and surfing their tantrum. Being reactive to the storm can become messy, but if you can put yourself in the eye of the storm, understanding the need, then this can help to eventually level the unrest and bring it back to calmness. Validating the anger and stress can also disperse it.

A client was screaming down the phone that their furniture did not fit. I could feel my fight or flight kicking in. But sitting with the awareness of my stress reaction to her anger voice meant I could let it be. The ability to separate emotionally from a person venting, protects the psyche with an emotional boundary. Over time, the more restraint used against confrontation, the more your personal resilience will increase.

Influencing the Mind to Uncover the Need

This section on influence will delve lightly into how the brain can have an influence on our needs and the awareness that is helpful in being receptive instead of reactive.

Influencing somebody so that you can uncover their needs involves many elements. Listening to the salesperson can be difficult when the noise of the environment and the design of the space can have an influence on their ability to feel comfortable The discomfort can restrict how much they are willing to reveal.

There is marketing research carried out on clients who had been given a warm cup of tea before going into a meeting and then repeated with clients given a cold drink. They found that the people holding the hot cup of tea were more open to suggestions than individuals with a cold drink.

The question of client comfort should also be on the mind when looking for the need of a customer. Questions such as "what can I give this person, how can I be of service" helps reciprocity in exchange for the opening questions that assist the trade.

We have to remember that we are talking about the emotional part of the brain when in conversation about the product. This section of the brain is there to protect the person from being taken advantage of and protects its boundary. Influencing people is not an easy task. There can be a fine line between trying to manipulate or inspire. Instigating reciprocity can create a necessary bond

People's ego state is very delicate. If somebody feels inadequate, they will put up barriers even if they are not sure it is needed. There is a theory that for every one negative comment you make to someone, it takes three positives to counterbalance it and regain an emotional equilibrium with the person. Therefore hurting somebody's ego means you have to plaster those emotional wounds with much more positive feedback to restore your trust.

When influencing a person's mood, you are becoming a conductor of the stress chemicals in their mind. You need to bypass the conscious thought process and communicate with the unconscious to find out what they are looking for within the mental entanglement. When the limbic part of the brain (the emotional brain) is activated, it will shut down communication with the neo cortex (the reasoning part of the brain). It is helpful to avoid any reactive drives from this section of the brain. Make sure you guide the mind back to the neo cortex so that the conversation can remain in a social environment rather than an insecure jungle environment. With a sense of safety in place, highlighting the need becomes a natural process of interaction.

Highlighting the need can also be done through showing. Using imagery of the product and physical demonstration can positively influence your audience. The more channels of communication you can involve, the more senses are activated. There are times where words can be tiring, and the ability to concentrate of the complexity of the syntax floats away. Becoming physically expressive in communication breaks up the process to help re-engage with your client. Even if you are selling something intangible, your use of gesture can give texture to a presentation.

A person's body can be a great indicator of whether they are with you on your sales journey or want to get off at the first available gap in your speech. There will be clues in people's physical experience to show whether you are allowed to ask more questions to reveal the need. Make sure you are always monitoring somebody's physical and energetic state as you progress in asking questions.

Questions that highlight needs gives better quality to your selling process. Keeping the mind focused and creative toward the need will hit set realistic targets. It is simple and effective, it just needs to be done.

- **Open questions are precious tools for investigation**
- **Create a tableaux of meaning**
- **Become an investigator of needs**
- **Prepare a question bank**

Yes and...

The true sign of intelligence is not knowledge but imagination.

Albert Einstein

'Yes and…' is a structure and technique that can help to keep connection with others. This simple but powerful tool supports the process of maintaining your mind in a creative outlook. It increases the ability to adapt to unexpected and overwhelming situations. Also, it lays the foundation for a playful mindset, a way to connect with people, sharing ideas and building on possibilities.

No matter how many times you may have rehearsed your sales pitch, life is unpredictable. We need to keep this energy of the unknown alive. Also creative thinking can give the opportunity to adventure into understanding ideas that were not accessible beforehand.

We are born into a very 'No' dominated culture. We have a tendency to be critical of other people's ideas. 'Yes and…' helps break down this longstanding tradition. 'Yes and…' means you are not competing, but instead gaining new understandings. In sales, the more that you can understand, while sustaining a playful nature with your client, the higher the chance of closing your deal. Even if the deal is not closed, rewards can come from these positive connections,
in the form of referrals or the return of your client wanting to deal only with you.

Why 'Yes, and…ing' is so helpful is because too often misunderstandings can come through communication. The ideas we have behind the words, its meaning based on personal experience and the tone that packs emotion into the word, can quickly become complicated to the person listening. The receiver has to interpret the meaning from their experiences to the words and be able to decipher the intention behind the words before returning answers.

This challenging journey can lead to confusion, misinterpretation, and resentment. That is why 'yes and...' means you can enter the home of another person's mind. It gives the chance to look at their design and furniture of the mental layout and then make decisions based on the gathered information. To verbalise an understanding of somebody's meaning is a form of listening that people hunger for on a daily basis.

What are you doing while you are listening to what a person is saying? Focusing on listening and finding agreement can give a magical interpersonal connection. Then you build on their point with your own. Your point should be a gift to that person, building on their original idea and adding value and creative possibilities to the initial perception.

Sometimes we get caught in the illusion that as adults we must restrict ourselves from play. We forget how energised people become when we playfully connect while building ideas. During the sales process if somebody is making a suggestion about a product that may be an objection 'yes and...ing' the objection can give a far greater chance of turning the objection into an agreement.

Playfulness puts the mind in the moment and also helps to bring positive chemicals into the brain, relieving unnecessary stress during the purchase.

Keeping the communication simple and to the point helps the mind remain clear. Giving too much information can lead to data overload, which can create uncertainty. This uncertainty can lead to, discomfort and frustrate the sales process.

Avoid Assumptions

"When you assume, you make an ass out of u and me." - Oscar Wilde

When you are building on ideas together with a 'yes and...' mindset, you can test assumptions that may appear from fragmented information. A mind full of assumptions can be disastrous for focusing on the need for the client. Instead of assumptions, searching for facts will diminish untruths and encourage a conversation with understanding.

It is also valuable to uncover people's assumptions of the product. They may not initially exist to the conscious. Communicating their assumptions out of the equation early on in the sales discussion buffers you for any rejection later on in the process. There is nothing worse than clients' assumptions coming crashing down emotionally into a sales interaction.

Connection

Understanding that ideas are everywhere, maintains the mind in a state of possibilities. Awareness of resistance and mental tension helps identify disconnection with others. As long as you stay relaxed and creative in the moment, most answers will come to you and dissolve the stress and reduce the fear.

I was once in a workshop where a participant decided not to do an exercise building on 'Yes and...' She said, "what is the point?" She had a very tight muscle structure around her face, and her eyes seemed to glaze over. Unfortunately, when you are in a negative haze, you don't even know that you are there. The ability to look out of it can only sometimes come with a shock or life disaster. She was unable to see the laughter and playfulness of the others and the value of the human connection. Not everyone is comfortable with creative thinking. It is your job to facilitate this by activating a gentle playfulness of the spirit.

'Yes and...' has empathy built into it and people like to feel compassion if they have something that is bothering them. 'Yes' has a profound vibration that is calming to the ear. Verbal confirmation that supports your understanding toward the client is where the empathy lies. The 'and' is a connection to that knowledge and the gifting and building of the conversation.

Yes to Yourself

Giving 100% of the best part of who you are, involves a level of vulnerability within your communication. This must be done while maintaining a level of self-care.

'Yes and...' also includes saying yes to yourself. Sometimes people are disrespectfully dumping their life issues on you, and they feel justified in doing so because "the customer is always right". Putting a boundary down is important for your self-care. Clients are not always right, and sometimes you have to know where your limits are. It's likely to be when your body is screaming to walk out of the deal. And it is probably best to do just that, walk. It can also flag up the potential headaches if there is going to be communication in the future with a client. Making this decision could avoid more grief than the commission is actually worth.

Listening

'Yes and...' is a simple technique that creates many possibilities. Just as the keys on the piano have a simplicity, their musical possibilities are endless. Keep in mind when things are simple, the energy is far more channeled.

Unfortunately, most of us are not in a 'yes and...' mindset which can cause all sorts of frustrations. I was once investigating purchasing leads for a start-up company. It was however beyond my budget at that time, but I observed how, as soon as the salesperson realised that I was outside of her business demographic, she cut me off.

That may be okay for her targets she had to hit for the week, but I would never go back to the company. A couple of minutes 'yes and...ing' to complete the transaction with a positive injection would keep the door open and seal a deal for the future.

'Yes and...' has that flexibility within story building. It opens up the blocked mind that believes all alternative thinking has been exhausted. This flexibility is like the straw in the water that does not break but bends to the gust of wind and bounces back to alignment. The simple 'yes and...' technique provides added strategies for your sales tool kit.

Riddles of a Challenge

The creative thinking mindset helps because sometimes solutions are not always that obvious, but with your brain looking at more possibilities, customer issues have a higher chance of being solved. I once had a conundrum with a power pack. Exchanged chairs were being sold off. The order that I sold should have but did not have a power pack inside the chair. Being new I began to panic because I knew a replacement took twelve weeks to order.

I could waste energy playing the blame game towards the delivery team but took on the responsibility to give an excellent service. Outside of wanting to do right by the client, there is also an NPS system in place that balanced everybody's wage with overall client feedback. One employees' bad score affected the whole team. I was being reminded of my responsibilities by the admin team. I was not sure what to do. Negative thoughts of self-talk began to insult my self-esteem, and I could feel emotions of fear and stress starting to block my brain.

One of the experienced sales staff had his mind in a 'yes and…' state. He was able to look at some old stock. He found a matching power pack. He removed the pack and gave it to me to drop off at the client on my way home.

I could then order another power pack within the twelve weeks for the old chair that meant everybody was happy. Replacing their power pack and giving them a bunch of flowers, left them satisfied. Shaking my hand when I left they promised to do more business with me in the future and loved the customer service.

The solution is always there, and the biggest problem was that I was unable to open up my creative process because of the chemical flooding of my brain. Practicing 'yes and…' can make creative thinking an habitual mindset to break through the chemical rush of stressful situations and help untangle the riddles of everyday challenges.

Creative Intelligence

We are animals of habit and continually revert to routine and scripted processes that give us a sense of security, but the routine can become a mental suffocation. 'Yes and…ing' situations can break these stale norms and lead you to connections that are not only innovative and varied, but make a mundane job much more colourful and enjoyable.

Albert Einstein said creativity is intelligence having fun. And this is what keeps you present, enthusiastic and vibrant.

One of the beautiful things about having this creative and flexible mind, is that when situations do not go to plan, you have the ability to bounce back. Misery comes when you board the train of despair by attaching yourself to a problem and allowing it to spiral down into an energy drain.

I believe once born every child is an artist. The challenge is holding onto that gift as insecurity, self-judgment and social conditioning begin to erode our creative inspiration. This erosion can happen in sales. Sales is an art form engaging the creative mind in the process of the moment and improvising within the now, so we need to work on keeping that creativity alive.

As mentioned before, the saying "we have two ears and one mouth, so we need to listen more than speak" is the foundation of your 'Yes and…ing' because you cannot build rapport without truly hearing. Stephen Covey quotes that "Most people do not listen with the intent to understand; they listen with the intent to reply." Too many of us are pre-guessing what a person is saying and start answering before that person's dialogue has finished. Understanding through listening creates time to build rapport, before you offer any advice.

To be heard as an individual, you may need to create a foundation of trust first to avoid being perceived as the typical sales person. As creatures of selective hearing, customers may also have a preconceived idea of what they are going to hear from you. Breaking this preconceived idea is possible by listening, as many people believe they will only be talked at when communicating with a sales professional.

Stories for the Mind

A great platform for creative thinking is the ability to create stories. For thousands of years, stories have inspired, educated and entertained and are a valuable tool for selling. They connect humans through their emotions and imagery, inviting people to join them in the world of their experience.

Stories create a feeling of emotional safety and help build people up psychologically from disastrous situations, like healing from grief. At certain times, stories are the only vehicle with the healing power to remove a thick cloud that's cloaking the mind. Stories give the ability for re-enacting emotional and intellectual challenges. Also, you can share the possibilities of the future, allowing the mind to open its imagination and experience different scenarios. These scenarios can expand the mind and escape the indecisive prison of choice.

People are attracted to stories which give them a sense of inclusion within our community. They are the social structure of childhood, and the imprinted archetypes dominate our well-being, which we tend to hold onto for as long as possible.

You may have started to tell a story and the other person walks away and may have found this immensely frustrating as you cannot resolve the tale and are left dangling, waiting for the conclusion.

Similarly, you may watch a movie that is not entertaining and have wanted to turn it off, but you end up forcing yourself to sit through it until it is finished. Again, this holding on is because you want to know the conclusion of the story, even if you already have a good idea how it will end.

Storytelling can be very useful in sales. If engaging enough, people have to hear to the end. The same is if they start to tell you a story. Allow them to complete it, to establish a sense of rapport. But of course, if they talk too much you may be allowing them to disturb your sales intension which is not useful. So a gentle easing out of the story in an appreciative and sensitive manner can help you get back on track.

Einstein mentioned he rarely thinks in words and I think that is a clue to connecting with our own personal "genius". If any sales person can tap into the imagery of thinking it would create a deep rapport as they open up to growing connection forming a shared tapestries of the mind.

Through universal enjoyment, stories level the status between individuals creating the same playing ground. Stories connect to the emotional mind, which generates more interest than any facts and numbers. People buy from people they know, like and trust, and stories are a great bridge into this world.

Modeling Stories

If you need to make a point through the communication of story, but you do not have the precise story to help with the situation, it is a good idea to take sections of stories and then sew them together into one.

I was selling some furniture where the customer was not sure if they wanted to pay for a service to stain protect their purchase. Their young children could stain and damage this investment and they were concerned. I share a stressful story that had happened to me a few weeks before. My little boy had found a blue crayon in his play box and marked the whole of the sitting room's cream carpet. I was in complete shock and had no idea what to do. I shared the core emotions behind the story, but instead of it being the carpet I transferred the story over to the furniture. The story had been modeled across which helped their decision to stain protect their purchase.

Metaphors

Metaphors are compelling images that enhance stories. The brain likes imagery that it can relate to and hold in its memory. For example to say:

This care box is good for removing stains.

or

The care box is your first-aid for spills and breaths life back into your fabric.

Using this form of communication activates the mind, focusing more attention on the possibilities while painting and charging the mental pictures with positive emotion.

A metaphor connects two universes of meaning which the brain likes to play with endlessly. This playfulness encourages the mind into a deeper understanding. The power of good metaphors is that they simplify meaning in a few words conjuring up an image that gives clarity to the conversation between people.

As memory can hold onto emotions and imagery far longer than words alone, the use of storytelling also gives the ability to share more information. Words, on the other hand, disappear faster in the brain dispersing them into minimal memory recall.

When creating a story, it is ideal to include plenty of sensory descriptions in your delivery, so that you can cover a wide range of possible sensory preferences. This sensitivity means if somebody has a slight preference for audio, visual or kinaesthetic language, they will be able to connect more immediately and deeply with your story.

Undercover No

'Yes and...' is not 'Yes but...'
'Yes but' is an undercover 'no' waiting to give up working on the person's idea. It seems that they are initially agreeing but in truth disregard your idea for theirs, which they believe is better. In a way, it can be more destructive that a clear 'no' because the initial yes opens up the individual's vulnerability and then the 'but' comes in to destroy the shared idea.

The person delivering 'yes but...' may think that they are listening, but the person receiving the information feels they are being attacked and starts to build barriers which close down the channel of healthy, trusting communication.

Also on a fundamental level 'yes' is more enjoyable than 'no' and the more it can be entwined into a conversation the more it will then encourage a yes mentality with everyone, which can also encourage more yeses for the sales.

To summarise, 'Yes and...' creates a flexible thinking process which in turn supports resilience. If you become an expert in searching for the possibilities of the conversation you have more chances of connection. This insight can prevent the exhaustion that can come from not knowing and trying to fight for your sale or desperately trying to hang on to a dying conversation. Flexibility creates many pathways to the same destination, unlike the locked mind that is a one-way road giving no room for maneuvering. The more you engage in this free thinking, the more natural and effective you will be, as you ride through the sea of stories and wo

- Maintain a healthy mind with a creative outlook
- 'Yes and…' helps reduce the tradition of argument
- Focus on listening
- Build on ideas

Training

You are your greatest asset. Put your time, effort and money into training, grooming, and encouraging your greatest asset.

Tom Hopkins

The cliché: "if you are not growing you are dying" can be just as valid for sales and your continued commitment to crafting and testing your skills, which in turn will keep you more alive in your daily interactions. Any development has some form of training behind it. Training to improve yourself has a greater chance of success when it comes from the heart. Forcing training onto people as a compulsory requirement is less likely to develop into fresh and effective new skills.

Understanding your reason for developing yourself and the 'why' you want to change or grow, will give you the energy and tenacity to complete the journey. The reward of the overall success is sometimes not enough when learning can have many obstacles on the way that may throw you off track. The ability to break each challenge into manageable units and celebrate the small successes, can carry a learner the distance needed.

It is important to monitor and measure the change. Many times when a change takes place, we find it hard to reconnect to the old behaviour. This illusion can leave you feeling that the change has not occurred. Being in a state of continual learning, brings excitement to your daily routines and tasks. This excitement and enthusiasm will, in itself, help attract and inspire clients.

Someone once asked me how long it takes to learn to become a professional dancer. I gave a number of 15 years. He was a horse trainer and said to become a great horse trainer takes 200 years. He says we have that number because the learning never stops.

I certainly feel this is true. The effort it took to create when I no longer wanted to learn anything new was immense. I knew that once I ceased wanting to improve as a dancer, this signaled the time for retirement. The excitement of progressing had previously given me endless energy and the physical fatigue was never a boundary.

To sustain your curiosity and keep your mind investigating the craft of selling, keeps you evolving within your industry.

Learning Strategy

Understanding your learning strategy helps because learning strategies can differ in relationship to your temperament. Trying to learn by an institutional learning formula which generates confusion in your mind, may lead to defining yourself as unintelligent. This struggle is more of a teaching disability than a learning one.

Knowing the way that you learn best, means that you can invest energy in structuring a learning strategy that will give you the same outcome with a personally modified approach. This awareness reduces the emotional navigating through failures that will come as you evolve.

I suffered for many years stumbling along with traditional ways of learning which – like learning by rote - is nothing but intense pain for my brain. When I came to realise that I was a visual learner, and not an audio learner, it meant I could change my approach to learning.

Information Retention

Starting a new job I had to retain product knowledge of hundreds of products. My adviser was trying to teach me through rote learning, which was producing weak results. Finally, I had to take the person to one side and explain that my memory and I work best with imagery. He let me be for a couple of hours and when he returned he was amazed by my ability to recall the information. My personal learning strategy took a little longer, but the retention of the information was far longer.

Keeping space in mind is essential for memory retention. Overcrowding can drown the brain with information. Repeating new information while expanding your subject means the learning effort is not wasted and retains the new info as you import the next stream of data. Test yourself continually as you go along so that you can measure what is sticking. This repetition will transfer learning from the short term memory to the long term.

If you have the support of others, it can be fun to do a presentation of your new information that you have learned. This playfulness helps take the memory out of your head and into daily life which embeds retention.

When first learning information, the way you formulated the learning can be the only way to recall it. It can help greatly to mix that information with other subjects that you are already confident with.

It can also be that there is not just one learning strategy for you, but several that resonate. By mixing these together, you can structure your learning style with different sensory ways of connecting to the knowledge.

There are also different stages of learning, and it is important to ride the change from conscious learning, like when a child is excited by its walking, to unconscious ability when concentrating on walking is no longer necessary. When I use learning before it becomes unconscious, there is a hesitancy in the communication that can be felt by clients. In order to be fully committed to your performance, your learning has to flow freely and build confidence with your listener. It is the constant drilling of a routine that finally embeds new learning into the unconscious.

For example, master the IT equipment that is there to help you with your sales process. If you end up fumbling around with technology because you are not yet competent with its functions, it takes you out of the flow. Not knowing which windows you need to get into creates hic-ups in your pitches and sends out a vibration of not knowing. The smoother you are with your tools, the more confidence your clients will have in you.

This hiccup happened to me when I first used a tablet at work. I remember getting stuck unable to move passed a window. This frustration was because I had to put a zero in one of the windows and it could not be left blank. The computer kept on beeping at me, and I was unable to connect with the client which led to my frustration and eventually her irritation. After that process, I decided to train myself on all the functions of the tablet. This drive was so that I would never find myself in that embarrassing situation again. I needed to become a specialist of my tool. All my concentration was on trying to perfect my sales technique, however I could not advance my sales skills without including the improvement of my tablet technique.

The Right Knowledge

It is important with training that you are doing the right training. Continually working hard for the sake of seeming dedicated, and rewarding yourself for your substance-less hard work, will be of no benefit, if it is the wrong knowledge.

Self-analysis is critical to the evaluation process of what you have chosen to improve on. First, figure out where you decide to put your energy and ensure it aligns with an outcome which is most beneficial to you.

Select and Reject

Adopt a 'select and reject' quality to your learning. This intervention can be done with speed, keeping you agile to change.

What you choose to select and reject is important. Keep the unwanted ideas for another time. Put the discarded parts into your memory banking system. This saving can be reused if necessary so that any learning's gathered from a new challenge may come in handy later. But for now, you select the most energetic and useful pathway to inform your learning.

Reflection

Reflection into action is a central part of activating learning. When reflecting on what has happened in a developing situation, you can also decide if it is beneficial to pursue action. In the learning process if the same strategy is implemented at least three times with the same result you are on the right pathway towards repeating and building on change.

Discovering a successful learning strategy is just as much part of the challenge as the learning of a subject. Sometimes people do not realise when they have found the correct strategy and continue to change it to the point it no longer works. Especially when the learning is new, you do not want to forget the parts that are working for you and watch them get muddled with the continual experimenting. It is like when you come to the end of an abstract painting having the ability to know when to stop is a major part of the artistic journey.

Dynamic reflection is critical during the sales process. In the moments of stillness, you can make mental notes of areas that are working and not what has worked previously. Later you can spend more time reflecting. By recreating the situation with mental markers, you can recall it later. After gathering the new learning, the next process is to place that knowledge into action. Then go through a 'select and reject' process again to refine your skill base.

Role-Play

Ability to rehearse your learning is also useful. If you find the person you feel comfortable with, role-playing your new learning can give you a chance to make mistakes. Also, you can build questions you may have forgotten about in your routine. The challenge with role-playing is that you can become self-conscious. Being aware you are performing can produce a sense of insecurity as you are worried that someone is monitoring you. This act may not give you the same flow that you would have had in a real situation, but acknowledging that this is a rehearsal gives time and place to test new ideas.

Training yourself to master your product knowledge means you can also understand the uniqueness of your product benchmarked against other products in the market. That can then be used to inform clients of the benefits of proceding with your sale. To know the benefits that your products can deliver, is the basis for leading to the close of the sale.

Knowing your new products inside out adds to a sense of trust from your client. If you can answer questions without hesitation, there is a sense you are an expert in your field. But also having the confidence to admit you do not know something, but are more than willing to go and get the answer and deliver it back to the person, also gives a sense of care and commitment.

Creating Value

Knowing your product means you can build on creating value stemming from the benefits of the item. I have witnessed with many people that the money itself is not an obstacle, but the salesperson has failed to illustrate enough value in the product, and therefore a spend of £10 suddenly feels like it was £100. At the same time, an item overpriced by £10 can feel like a bargain if the value has been emphasised.

Being a specialist in you products gives you more chance of creating value. Product knowledge also gives you authority. People feel in safe hands when somebody knows their 'stuff'. When you establish your badge of specialism you will earn their trust. People will start asking you for your advice and believe that you will lead them in the right direction. This knowledge can also differentiate the value of the products you are selling.

An Outside Eye

Learning is not just an individual experience. Much of learning happens in the moment. Taking those moments and then asking for advice from people that are successful in the areas that you wish to become better in, will help you grow. Shared learning within a group can be very empowering growing together to improve skills and rapport as a team.

Having a coach and expert as the observer of weaknesses and strengths can give additional insight where you may be limited. This observation can speed up learning immensely. We all have blind spots in our psyche and an outside expert can challenge us in particular areas we may not wish to visit, but to get to the next stage of our development, we have to face that challenge head-on.

Keeping the mind active and alert with researching sales techniques online, in books and from experts, will generate new discoveries. But it is not an intellectual game. Mobilise yourself from a dreamlike state of sales philosophy. The knowledge has to be borne out in experience and through that experience you can monitor growth.

- Break each challenge into manageable units
- If we're not growing, we are dying
- Understand your learning strategy
- Rehearsal creates confidence

Humour

Humor is a leveler. It brings us back to the human level.

Swami Beyondananda

Humour is a powerful way to connect with people. It produces a sense of friendship as you link through shared meaning. There is an understanding between people who laugh together. Humour creates a feeling of ease when a group is sharing positive laughter. It can help you survive some of the most mundane days of your life and be a driving energy through obstacles.

Placed in the right moment, humour can also be a white flag in a conflict. It can create a sense of playfulness that stimulates positive chemicals in the brain. On the shadow side, it can be a delicate line between bonding and 'bitching' which can create a negative divide within a social group.

Negative humour points out a person's flaws and drills repetitively to get an easy laugh at the victim's expense. This type of humour is bullying disguised by laughter. Also, people's pain can be cloaked in humourous attacks, taking attention away from sales and directing the group's attention onto others. Banter can be an excuse for negativity. There can be the idea that if you cannot handle banter, you might be weak. But I've also seen banter used behind people's backs, sales professionals talking endlessly about another person, but smiling to their face. This type of humour lacks internal integrity and can cause dysfunctional office politics.

The challenge of negative humour is that your team's emotional environment also reflects on the work that you achieve. If you are unable to guard yourself against negative comments drilling inside your psyche, you can find it hard to get your mind in the game. It can also be a tool used by the disreputable sales person with an intention to get into your head through the disguise of humour to gain a competitive edge.

Healthy competition sprinkled with humour can be beneficial for a team. My manager once asked the sales team to work in groups, and we competed to beat the other team's numbers. The day resulted in the overall store numbers going up. But the idea was not evaluated, and groups returned to their individual fighting for targets. There was a magic in the shared fun as the groups laughed and joked between their rivals. On the individual sales level, it became more cut-throat with lower allover results.

The Sensitive Smile

A positive aspect of humour is when you can laugh at many challenging situations. This smiling ability shows that you have a sense that the big picture is in a process and focusing in on the struggle is only a temporary problem. A laugh indicates that on the other side everything will be okay. It is a form of optimism that can be of benefit to a team.

Monitoring the reaction of somebody you are laughing 'at' is a necessary sensitivity. Laughing 'at' also needs to include laughing with people. If the person you are laughing at is getting stressed, you need to stop because this behaviour quickly transforms into a form of abuse. Maintaining a conscious awareness can prevent getting lost in a "group mind" that becomes high on their positive chemicals, but blind to their negative impact.

Humour is a Funny Thing

Engaging with someone trying hard to be funny can become very uncomfortable. Pushing laugher onto people can become a repellant to your relationship. A few decades ago during a comedy course in New York, I experienced this discomfort. The receptionist was an inspiring comic, but every sentence that left his month conveyed a desperate need to be funny. This forced manner was more about his cleverness than building rapport together. He saw himself as the deliverer of comedy and misunderstood the communication and connection of comedy. He became more annoying than funny, and I did my best to avoid him in the mornings.

That is the delicacy of working with a client, and forcing humour can distance somebody instead of bonding with them.

A few techniques:

Explain the pain can be a way of creating laughter.

I like to share decorating stories with couples that are doing up their house. To get a humourous connection, I would revert to my pain when doing up my first house. I refer to the advert in the 90s where the couple is happily painting the halls and giggling as they splashed each other with paint. "I never had the Dulux experience; mine was working long hours into the night disagreements on the work, frustrations, and annoyances, but at the end of that journey we had a wonderful home for our new family that also made a significant profit."

In this example, I present the reality of doing your home up in contrast to the fantasy, and that although it is challenging, the final result is worth every moment.

Exaggeration within humour

I asked customers if they have been looking long for their product. If they say yes with an exhausted look, I then exaggerate the recognition.

"You have that look of shopping overwhelm, a little battered and confused with too much choice... You need a hot drink and at last your journey has come to a satisfying end and all that stress has resulted in the decision that is right for you. Tea or coffee? Clients tend to laugh at the exaggeration of the suffering, but concluding that the pain is over, produces a happy smile.

A reliable tool for humour is to add a slight exaggeration to somebodies humorous comment. If you continue to heighten the suggestion the laughter can grow and continue to get funnier. But this type of humour-building is also delicate, because if the exaggeration is too great, you lose connection with the person you are building with and creates a disconnect. Also if you go off on a tangent, you can seem self-indulgent. This type of humour is like playing a game, and if you keep the ball only in your court, the game is over.

Callbacks are a crafted form of exaggeration used when you have had a laugh at a subject, and later on, on a different topic, you bring back the same laughter with a new twist. This interactivity shows a sense of intelligence to your language integration and also demonstrates that you have been listening. This inspired laughter continues to deepen the bond.

Laughter

Another reason for promoting sales that accentuate our natural need for human interaction, is that it creates a sense of happiness. In a society that is suffering from a culture of overwork and stress, moments of laughter help us reconnect to the present.

There is a misconception that happiness is waiting at the end of a successful adventure. But happiness is an emotion, not a goal. This emotion activates your choice in a moment. It is in this simplicity that it can give meaningfulness to a sales interaction.

If it is happiness that we strive for, then let us include it in our daily lives.

People who tend to have a happy demeanor tend to have the ability to bounce back from difficulties in life. Happiness opens up our mind to optimism and the more optimistic you can be the more avenues to close the sale are available to your thought process.

Laughter, the effect of good humour, comes in "two forms", according to Sophie Scott. There is the inner gut animal type laughter that can almost sound like a mating baboon and is very primal. This kind of laughter can have a wonderful resonating feeling to the body for the rest of the day. The other type of laughter is based on social agreements. A forced laugh to acknowledge agreement with the person is a form of connection. These, although different kinds of laughter, have their place and it is important to recognise the differences between them.

Also, happiness influences certain chemicals in the brain such as dopamine, oxytocin, serotonin to endorphins. These chemical cocktails put us into a sense of well-being and help us to overcome many emotional challenges. Small moments of bonding activates a sense of closeness to somebody. This closeness releases these positive chemicals and a sense of happiness will follow.

The release of endorphins can reduce the stress hormone cortisol that stimulates 'Fight or Flight.' Deane Alban, from Be Brain Fit, states that chronically elevated cortisol is linked to lowered immune function, obesity, high blood pressure, insomnia, and heart disease. It also contributes to brain fog, anxiety, depression, mood swings, memory loss, concentration problems, and mental disorders of all kinds.

The health benefits of laughing expand the lungs and stretch the muscles in the body giving the body a positive workout. Just some of the advantages of humourous interactions with clients.

Humour does not need to be a standup gig drowning in heaps of laughter. It can be subtle and be a gift even in the way you say hello in the morning with a slightly different way than expected. Simple contrast can be a pleasant surprise. These subtle connections can drip into your daily interactions and hydrate the foundation of humour throughout the day.

People who lead conversations with their wounds and decide to open up by moaning are sometimes described as emotional vampires. Their lack of sleep, relationship issues, life direction or whatever wounds are pressuring them, spill out of their consciousness and form their daily misery into dialogue. There is a choice to make, wallow in self-pity or live in the possibilities of the moment? Which choice is more generous to your wellbeing?

The Contagious Smile

Humour is also activating facial expressions such as smiling. From a very young age, the smile of an adult is our primary form of communication informing us that we are safe. Adult smiling is an attractive expression that draws people closer to you. As an adult, a shared smile is still a sign that this person is safe to approach.

If your first interaction with a client is met with an authentic smile, you have a higher chance of being allowed to get closer when they are showing interest in the products.

Humour also indicates that you are not taking yourself too seriously and breaks the stereotype of a pushy sales person. This preconceived idea can be diluted with a smile, laugh or expressing a sense of happiness.

Victor Borge quotes "laughter is the shortest distance between two people." That is what you are looking for, to break down the barriers so that you can connect and advise based on the need that has been shared with you.

Sales can be an emotional rollercoaster of a ride, and if taken too seriously, it will start to punish you. At the end of the day, if your selling has not reached the target you had hoped for, but the human connection with your customers has created a sense of well-being, you are in a better place to start fresh the next day.

Using humour in your sales pitch can break up the repetitive nature of sales. It can reduce the feeling that you are selling one product after the next, instead of focusing on each personality. It gives the client a chance to relax and digest the benefits of the product. Giving space, also keeps the connection and prepares the foundation for any other sales information you wish to share.

- **Connect through humour**
- **Bullying disguised as humour, breaks team spirit**
- **The emotional environment affects results**
- **Laugh at countless challenging situations**

Mindset

Life isn't about finding yourself. Life is about creating yourself.

George Bernard Shaw

The most important thing in sales is your mindset. If your mind is not in the right place you won't be selling very much. When your head's gone, your sales numbers drop.

In this chapter of Mindset I will share examples of how I shifted my own mindset and how critical this was for increasing and maintaining my sales targets.

A Need to Sell

Too often our lack of the right knowledge put into action can create the greatest barriers. If somebody asked me when I was in the arts if making money was important to me, I would have replied with a vague yes. The vagueness would be because I had more of an intellectual understanding of money, than any particular or focused mindset.

Now I look back and see how far away I was from increasing my income. When I visit my friends from my old Arts industry, I listen to how they speak and I can hear from their language, that they will not be attracting significant money into their life. That was the language I used to use, until my environment shifted from The Arts to Sales, and dragged me out of an old way of thinking.

Previously I was happy to swim in the thought process of creativity. To connect with artists building on ideas and forming imagination into reality, was a wonderful place to be. As an educator my main focus was on the support of the learning mind, so my energy was invested in others under the security of my paycheck.

When it came to the time to make the jump and start my own company, I was enthusiastic about the independence and self reliance of making my own profit. However the skills of an established artist, an effective educator and a successful coach, were not enough. And the inability to understand sales and marketing resulted in the inability to find a sustainable drive and focus towards money, which meant that I was unable to get my business off the ground.

The mental suffering that resulted from my inability to put money on a higher placed value system was immense.

I have attended the workshops in NLP to transform my relationship to money and other forms of change work. I became conscious that money was not high on my value system. But no matter how many types of exercises I undertook, my mental value towards money did not shift. I even went back into my childhood to understand my relationship with money within my family. Despite intellectually understanding the workings of money, I couldn't really feel it in my bones.

Then I entered the field of retail and the daily conversations with my peers were dominated by money. They had financial goals for every day, every week, every month – even the year. It was all about the numbers, how to make the deal whether it was a couple of pounds or thousands of pounds. I found a difference from my previous environments that were more about philosophy. But in sales many of the staff members are there to make money and this is the sole motivator. What you are selling does not matter, as long as the numbers piled up in your bank account.

This obsession with numbers meant you watched your numbers daily. We would print out our KPIs that monitor our gains and failures, we would look at our delivery's constantly to see how much we had to push by the end of each week. When I had a social chat with my colleagues I had to have one eye on the door, so as not to miss the next client and ensure their money lined my pocket and not those of my sales colleagues.

This was the foundation for my neurological re-structure. After years of being embedded in the sales environment, I could sense that my demeanor had changed. When I thought about the most important things in my life, money was now up their with creativity, performance, learning and contribution. I was able to reframe some of the most important elements linked to learning and family with money. Having a healthy income brought more opportunities of growth.

It is important to understand where your drive comes from. I was told by people that drive came from wanting to have a house, go on holiday, changing life. It doesn't matter what it is, as long as it resonates deep with your core needs.

My drive came from a need to succeed. I had to educate myself in the art of sales, so that when I launched my own company for the second time, I was in a stronger place. This drive placed my focus on what is necessary.

Get Going

I learnt an interesting lesson from an award-winning business woman on the Isle of Wight. I asked her how did you get to owning a successful business in Bed and Breakfast? She said it began with scones.

Her B&B building had not been completed and she needed to get an income. She knew that she was good at making scones and people would pass her building on long country walks. The kitchen was ready and a small place to have a few tables and chairs to eat. She managed to start her income by selling scones and tea. This led to her completing the building and having a successful Bed and Breakfast business.

So her advice to me was figure out how much money you want to make and just get going, no matter how basic at the start, just bring in the money.

In order for the drive to have enough energy behind it there needs to be a limitation on your focus. Just like the magnifying glass will, with precisely the right amount of sunlight directed to a flammable object, creates fire. The mind will do the same. The problem is it can be very slippery and concentration becomes splintered. With more than three ideas, the energy it takes to build money can be radically diminished.

Always be Closing

The age old saying ABC Always Be Closing is a strong reminder to keep the mind focused on your intention. The question is how do you keep your mind on always closing? In the RHYTHM Sales Method the closing must be the end goal, but the close organically evolves within your relationship following your first interaction. The closing of a deal is behind everything: your listening ability, gaining trust, highlighting the need and sharing a laugh with your customer, to the point where they ask for the deal. And if these interactions don't result in the client asking you, you have at least created the best possible atmosphere to ask for the deal yourself without seeming pushy.

They ask for the deal or you do. That's the endgame.

Mindfulness

In order to have a defined mindset it is helpful to practice mindfulness.

The word mindfulness is sometimes misunderstood as sleepy or somehow controlling the mind. This is a misconception of the benefits of the practical application of mindfulness used in the sales environment. As sale professionals can struggle to keep their minds in the sales zone, the antidote is mindfulness training. The mind can be very slippery and internal dialogue can become unhelpful and negatively repetitive.

This type of mindfulness creates a mental observer who monitors where the mind fixates and limits itself. If for years unhealthy thought processes pollute your brain and negative patterns get in the way of development, it is time to let them go. To untangle this process it takes the same type of dedication that you would need to build up muscles in a gym. But instead of using forces to create strength, you increase awareness and acceptance with strength and resilience coming from not forcing.

The dedication and change is based on your commitment to time for yourself, something people can have a hard time doing. Making a choice to allow the time for this training is not something that comes lightly in the busy world that we live in.

The cloud of your personality has to disappear so that you are able to listen to your gut feeling with more courage and precision. By doing this you are able to communicate honestly with yourself. Inner honesty gives life direction and with this clarity comes increased energy.

Meditation each day is the same as going for a run for a marathon runner. You have to constantly practice your awareness or you revert back to your original state. It is in the continuity of mind practice that you begin to gain a mental shift that creates a sense of freedom within your thought processes.

Much of life is focused on the external, missing the balance between your inner world and the outside world which can be draining. Taking time to listen to your breath seems airy. But if someone was to take away your airways to life it would be very serious within a few minutes.

Constantly looking for distractions to cover up the noise that in your head, can take you away from what is important. These distractions with their addictions can take time to shift, but doing so can move forward your mindset.

It is the moment to moment awareness that you are trying to perfect. The ability to be aware of your environment, such as the soundscape of your workplace, puts you in the present moment. The more time we spend in the present moment, the lighter life becomes.

The more you can strip away your negative thought process the more resilience you can have in daily life. At times the sales process does not go well. This can lead to spiraling into a pit of self pity. Becoming aware of the change in your emotional state, means you have a better chance of shifting it before your thoughts destroy your sales for the rest of the day.

This type of mind training is useful because when you are in the negative state - and sometimes not even aware that you are there, you wind yourself up. The stress from this wind up can be felt by your client. Although you feel that you are doing your routine job, your energy is pulling away from your possible earning potential.

I have seen countless times when sales people start off with a bad deal and it gets into their psyche. Then the rest of the day is written off. This activates a snowball effect where they start to create a belief system that polices an imprisoned idea that they cannot sell. It does not take long before the idea becomes a reality, and that reality matches the stuck thought process. It takes a pattern break to dislodge the mind to release its grip on this belief system. This can help the mind revert back to a more professional mindset needed to sell well.

With negative thoughts put aside, it allows for a more direct focus on your skills rather than your worries and concerns. Also obstacles can be taken at face value, free from past attachments to them. Too much of our time is spent making judgments on our personal talent linked to past achievements. Past achievements are in the past and you are not the same person you were yesterday, therefore getting on with it and dealing with the moment is more important than drowning in the past or being anxious about the future.

There was a time where personal challenges were affecting my sales numbers. I tried to push through the day doing my job, but my mind was poisoned. That's when I decided to take on a mindfulness training. After two months I could feel myself evolving. My colleagues were saying that I had become more focused. One of the things with these types of internal growth spurts, is that it's more your outside environment that will notice the change before you do. As I started to clear out my unnecessary and unhelpful thoughts, my numbers began to shift for the better.

So for me, mindfulness is not a new age form of spiritual fantasy, but a pragmatic way to achieve change to make a difference to your sales numbers and in turn those numbers make a difference to your income.

The stress of selling can be reduced by taking the time to stop and reconnect to a thought process that elevates your wellbeing.

Taming the mind can be achieved by simply observing it, and it is in this clarity of thinking that more energy for success can be harnessed. If we increase our consciousness, we can create a selling process that is more compassionate towards ourselves and our clients.

Test mindfulness for a few months in relation to your mindset and observe how relationships and outcomes start to change for the better.

- **Get going**
- **Make a commitment to your time**
- **Clear the clouds of your personality**
- **Let it be**
- **Train the mind daily**

PETER ANDERSON

Summary

Life is about rhythm. We vibrate, our hearts are pumping blood, we
are a rhythm machine, that's what we are.

Mickey Hart

Living in a time when the idea of long-term security in employment
is disappearing; more people are becoming self-employed; and contract
work is at an all time high, learning the art of sales could not be more
important. If we are to be living in a sales-based society, how do we
wish to conduct ourselves? Will we desperately push for deals or hide in
the hope that everything will be ok? Can we create wonderful
connections with people in an exchange of service that not only fulfills
individual needs but also creates a sense of well-being?

Although RHYTHM is an acronym that covers the structure of the
RHYTHM Sales Method, it is not a linear process. Mindset is based on
your overall mental state and starts from when you wake up in the
morning. Too many of us wake for a moment and see the morning
light, but then the brain kicks in and we quickly disappear back into our
distractions and return to a dream state while still awake.

Becoming more present helps the other processes fall organically
into place. This creates an attractive energy that makes people feel
comfortable around you which in turn, leads to more meaningful
relationships. This can be a natural process. The challenge is quieting all
the mental noise that we create from past experiences and freeing the
present from the judgements that come from these.

We need to have an awareness of any mind discomfort in our social interactions. Once we have this we can chose to free our mind of these thought pollutants and enter into successful business communications. This clarity of mind will help gain trust, build rapport and shared meaning which is a great foundation for open dialogue and helps to highlight the needs of our clients.

Sometimes it can feel like a great effort to engage with people. Keeping our creative minds nimble, steers us away from the lethargic mindset that drags people away from the face to face interaction of a successful sales encounter. Another benefit of creative thinking is as the digital age shifts and changes happen at high speed, having a creative thought process that embraces a 'yes and..' mindset will help keep your work relevant in an unstable economy. This flexibility of mind helps you adapt to the appropriate style of sales interaction required at any given moment

In these changing times, we need to be in a forever learning mindset and constantly evolving. This learning needs to be measured so that we can repeat and overcome areas of weakness and gain a sense of mastery of our chosen subject.

However, if this method bogs you down trying to put everything together, you have to remember the element of humour and a good sprinkle of giggles can take learning a long way. The less we get locked into perfection and enjoy the process, the more open our minds become and remain. This playful manner keeps life light and agile, aiding effective learning. If we can crack a smile in the most difficult times, it becomes far easier in our daily interactions.

Staying centered while selling helps grow our financial security with a sense of satisfaction. The practice of mindfulness selling will incorporate itself in many aspects of your life, as sales is a constant in our daily interactions. We sell to our kids, to our partners, friends, and family. We have to sell ideas, needs, and change throughout our lives, so it is best to find a way of doing it that is motivated by human connection.

The definition of sales tends to emphasise the exchange of a commodity for money. I think that it is a limited definition because you can find sales inspiration where there is no money exchange. Like the boys' dance project I directed in schools, I was able to convince them to dance in front of their school after seven hours of training. This would be an experience of a lifetime and tap their creative potential. Getting this commitment from the boys was achieved through selling. And at the time I was using the RHYTHM method intuitively without realising what I was doing. It just felt natural, authentic and gained amazing results.

Different types of personalities will be attracted to different kinds of sales methods. RHYTHM Sales Method can help the sales newbie, but also the veteran sales professional who is missing targets and needs to understand their psychological mindset in order to get back in the game effectively.

RHYTHM Sales Method is the amalgamation of over three decades of coaching, educating, performing and selling creative ideas, paintings, property and furniture.

I've been inspired to create this approach and process after working with many sales professionals who struggled to stay in a healthy mindset. Selling is said to be all in the head and this is largely true. However, a more holistic understanding of the mind, mindset and well being, beyond just the intellectual and strategic, opens up enormous possibilities for creativity and growth. Most importantly we can learn to simultaneously improve our lives and close the deal.

Appendix

Suggested Next Steps

As with all meaningful shifts in behavior, to reap the rewards we need to translate intellectual understanding into implementation and change. I've suggested a simple pathway to help with this process (Fig.1). Each step is explained below and I encourage you to log your activity in the pages provided.

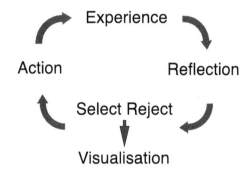

Fig.1

Explanation of Training Cycle

Experience – Description of event

e.g. I am selling a painting.

Reflection – Observations and self–analysis

e.g. I made assumptions that the client would not like a painting and was incorrect. I need to allow the client to express their interest and not push what I believe to be their interest.

Select and Reject – Select what you want to work on and reject anything unnecessary or unhelpful

e.g. I need to work on listening and exploring the clients' interests more. I can relax and create more space and silence for this to be possible.

Visualisation – Create a mental image of the desired outcome

e.g. I saw myself listening and the clients being very animated in their conversation

Action – Do it!

e.g. I started to reverse the balance and dynamic of my dialogue with clients. They talk and I listen.

Experience

_____

_____

_____

Reflection

_____

_____

_____

_____

_____

Select

_____

_____

_____

Reject

_____

_____

_____

Visualisation

_____

_____

Action

_____

_____

Experience

_____

_____

_____

Reflection

_____

_____

_____

_____

Select

_____

_____

_____

Reject

_____

_____

_____

Visualisation

_____

_____

Action

_____

_____

Experience

_____

_____

_____

Reflection

_____

_____

_____

_____

_____

Select

_____

_____

_____

Reject

_____

_____

_____

Visualisation

_____

_____

Action

_____

_____

Contact

To start a conversation about what RHYTHM Sales can do for you, please get in touch with Peter at:

peter@rhythmsales.com

www.rhythmsales.com

or his LinkedIn account at:

https://www.linkedin.com/in/peterandersonrs